SOURCEBOOK OF ELEGANT HISTORIC ORNAMENT

Emile Leconte

and

Charles Ernest Clerget

DOVER PUBLICATIONS, INC.
New York

Bibliographical Note

This Dover edition, first published in 1995, is an unabridged republication of *Mélanges d'Ornemens* [sic], as described in the Publisher's Note, which was written specially for the present edition.

DOVER *Pictorial Archive* SERIES

Library of Congress Cataloging-in-Publication Data

Leconte, Emile.
   [Mélanges d'ornemens. English]
   Sourcebook of elegant historic ornament / Emile Leconte and Charles Ernest Clerget.
      p.   cm. — (Dover pictorial archive series)
   "Unabridged republication of Mélanges d'ornemens [sic]"—Copr. p.
   ISBN 0-486-28709-2 (pbk.)
   1. Decoration and ornament—Plant forms—Europe. 2. Decoration and ornament—Plant forms—Middle East. I. Clerget, Charles Ernest, 1812–1875? II. Title. III. Series.
NK1560.L3613 1995
745.4—dc20
                                        95-32794
                                          CIP

Manufactured in the United States of America
Dover Publications, Inc., 31 East 2nd Street, Mineola, N.Y. 11501

PUBLISHER'S NOTE

THE NINETEENTH CENTURY was the great era of the design sourcebook. An early (and rare) example is the work reproduced here, *Mélanges d'Ornemens* [sic], drawn and engraved by Charles Ernest Clerget and published, apparently in installments, by Emile Leconte, Paris, ca. 1837. (Many of the plates were printed in two or three colors; here they are reproduced in black and white.)

Little is known of Leconte, but Clerget (1812–1875?), a sub-librarian at the Union Centrale des Beaux-Arts Appliqués à l'Industrie, was also known for book illustration and decoration. His output varied from illustrations for a work on mineralogy, and 150 plates for the Muséum d'Histoire Naturelle, to drawings for Gobelins tapestries and Sèvres ceramics.

The captions to the plates are based on the original and, although identifications are sketchy at best, the high quality of the engravings makes them of considerable interest to artists and designers.

PLATE 1: Original title page.

PLATE 2:   Details, seventeenth century.

PLATE 3: Foliate motifs, after sixteenth-century designs.

PLATE 4:   Ornaments, style of the sixteenth century.

PLATE 5:   Details for damascening.

PLATE 6:   Carpet, after Persian designs.

PLATE 7:   Motifs.

PLATE 8: Details, sixteenth century.

PLATE 9:   Field and border.

PLATE 10: Sixteenth-century niellos.

PLATE 11:   Original part title.

PLATE 12: Wallpaper decoration.

PLATE 13: Rosettes.

PLATE 14:   Foliate designs after Virgil Solis, sixteenth century.

PLATE 15: Details.

PLATE 16:   Ceiling design.

PLATE 17: Tapestry and embroidery.

PLATE 18:   Carpet.

PLATE 19:   Arabesques after Ducerceau.

PLATE 20:   Motifs, style of the sixteenth century.

PLATE 21:   Rosette and vignettes after Virgil Solis, sixteenth century.

PLATE 22: Details after Théodore de Bry, sixteenth century.

PLATE 23:   Field and border.

PLATE 24:   Blind or screen.

PLATE 25:   Motifs after Théodore de Bry, sixteenth century.

PLATE 26: Ornaments from the Alhambra.

PLATE 27:   Persian designs.

PLATE 28:   Vignettes, various styles.

PLATE 29: Fields.

PLATE 30: Carpet.

PLATE 31:   Rosette and panels.

PLATE 32:   Field and details, style of the Alhambra.

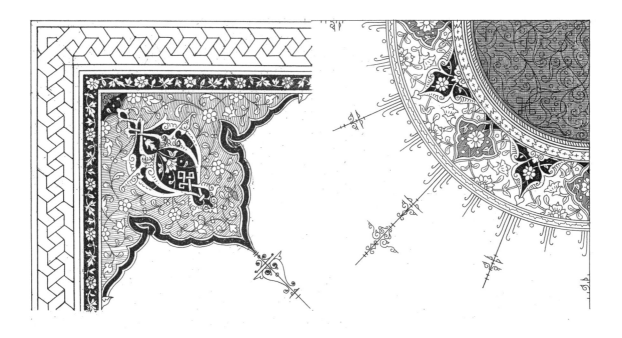

PLATE 33:   Persian details.

PLATE 34: Motifs for damascening.

PLATE 35: Field and border.

PLATE 36: Carpet.

PLATE 37: Title-page design, used as part title.

PLATE 38: Damascening designs, sixteenth century.

PLATE 39: Wallpaper and borders.

PLATE 40: Arabic rosette.

PLATE 41:   Arabesques after a Greek manuscript.

PLATE 42:   Arabian carpet.

PLATE 43:   Miscellaneous, after Daniel Hopper, Adrian Collaert, Ducerceau and others.

PLATE 44:   After Watteau, eighteenth century.

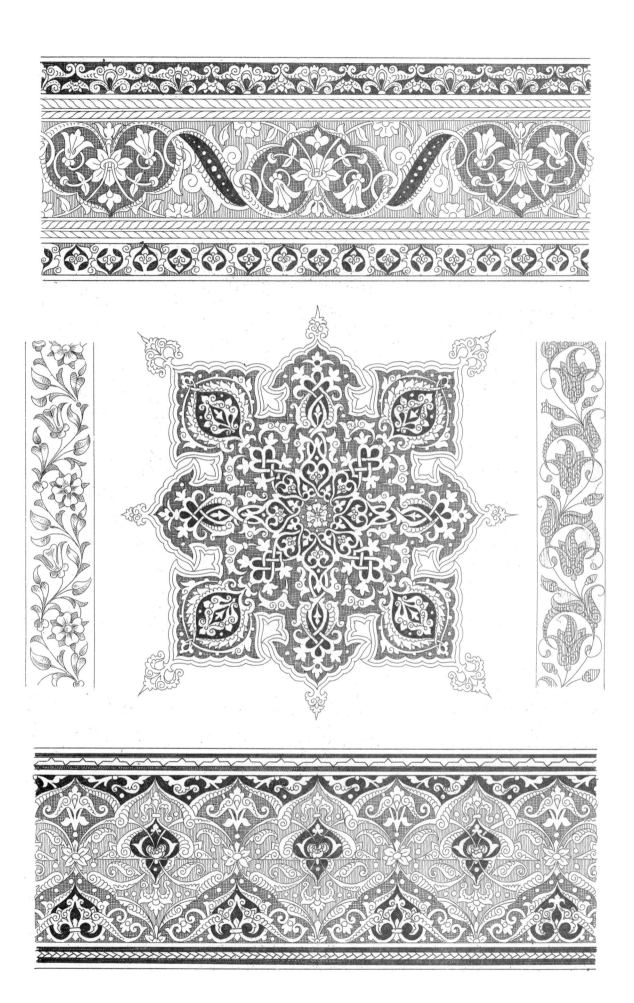

PLATE 45: Details taken from Persian manuscripts.

PLATE 46:   Renaissance vase and motifs.

PLATE 47:   Field, style of the seventeenth century.

PLATE 48:   Blind in the Gothic style.

PLATE 49:   Gothic title design, used as part title.

PLATE 50:   Motifs after Heinrich Aldegrever.

PLATE 51: Sixteenth-century designs.

PLATE 52:   Wallpaper designs.

PLATE 53: Persian designs.

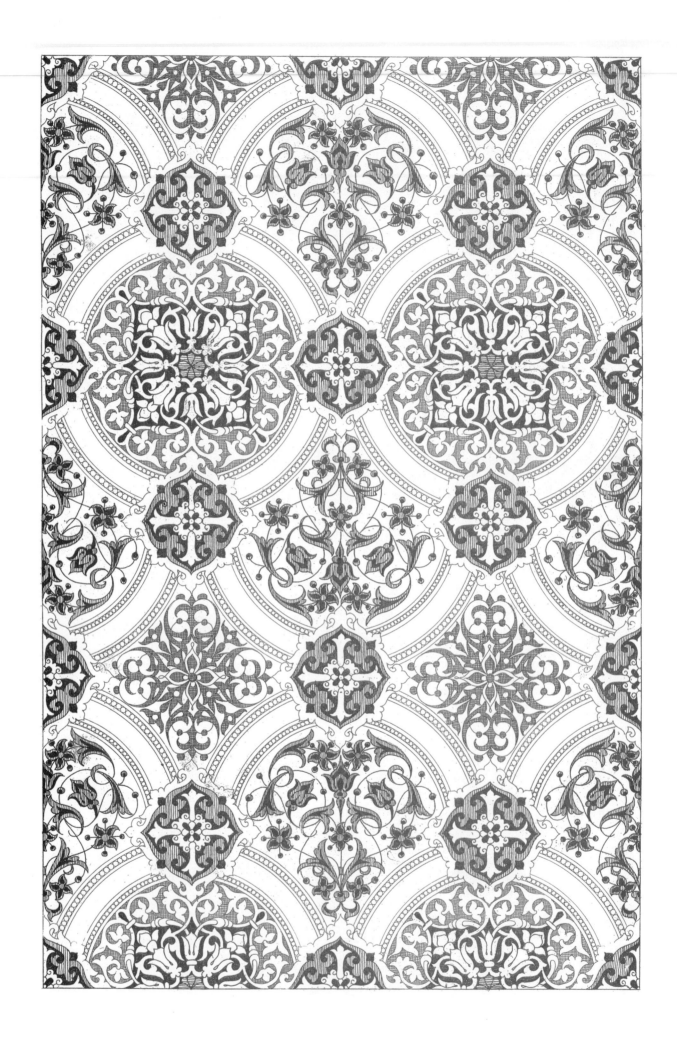

PLATE 54: Field.

PLATE 55:   Part title to the tenth installment.

PLATE 56:   Motifs for inlays.

PLATE 57:   Section of a decoration.

PLATE 58: Rosette.

PLATE 59: Friezes.

PLATE 60:   Designs for tapestry.

PLATE 61: Motifs after Agostino Veneziano (Agostino dei Musi), sixteenth century.

PLATE 62:   Panels and border.

PLATE 63:   Borders and frieze.

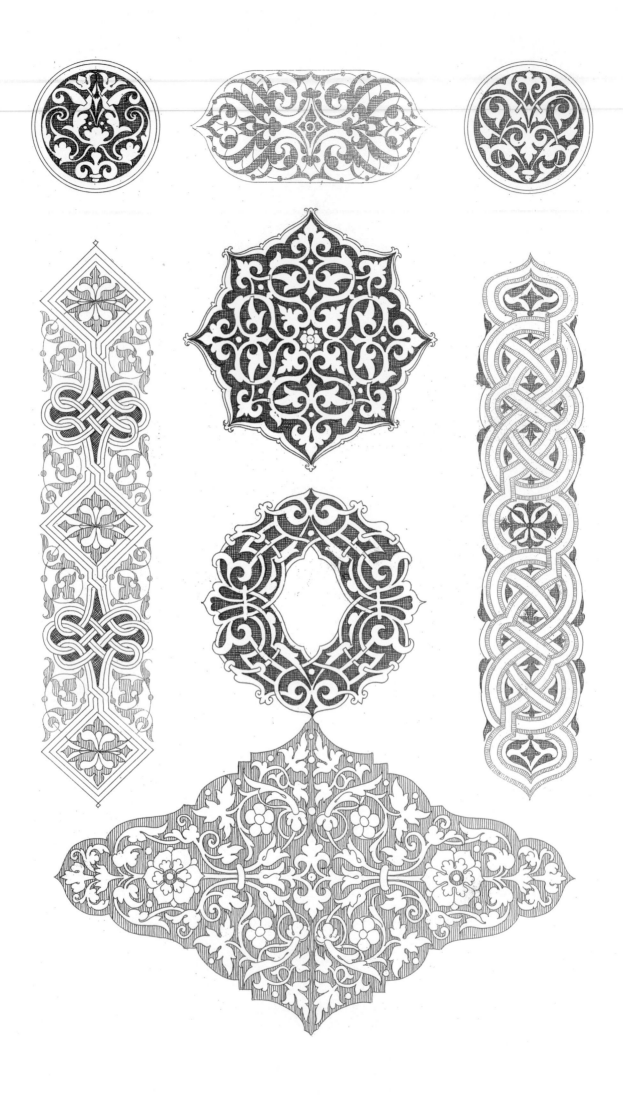

PLATE 64: Various vignettes.

PLATE 65: Field and border.

PLATE 66:   Field and border.

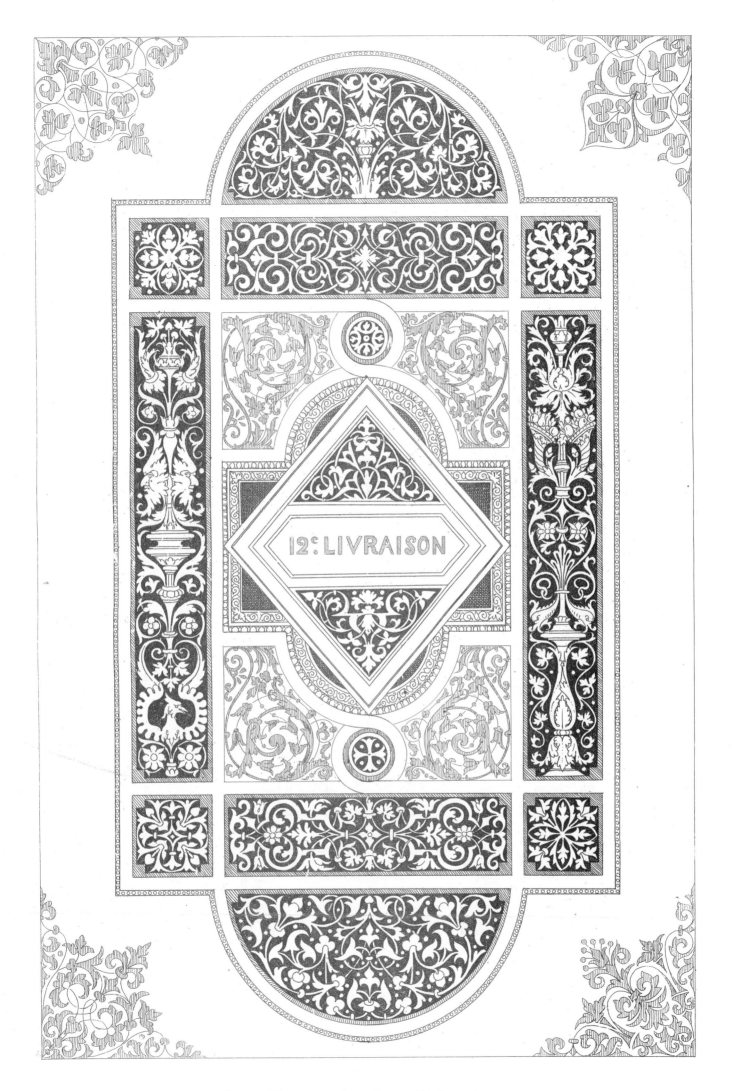

PLATE 67: Part title to the twelfth installment.

PLATE 68:   Rosettes.

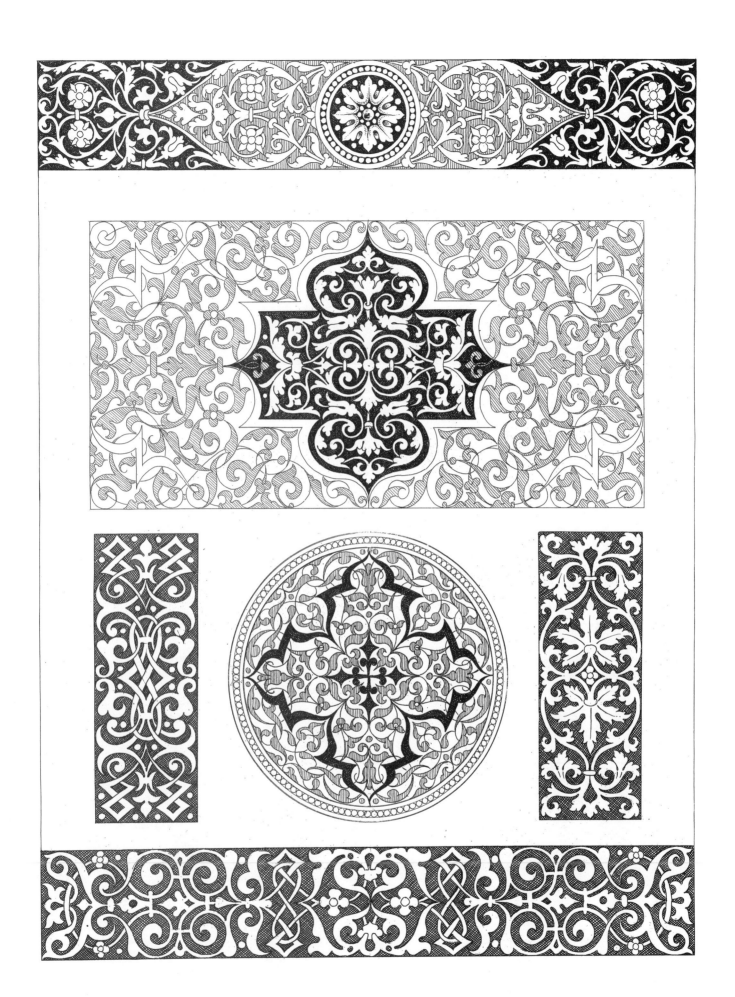

PLATE 69: Various vignettes.

PLATE 70:   Field and border.

PLATE 71:   Foliate designs.

PLATE 72: Arabic design.